CELTIC ART

By Harry Adès

Designed by Tony and Penny Mills

CELTIC
ART

This edition published and distributed by Tara, 1999

Reprinted in 2000

Tara is an imprint of Parragon

Parragon
Queen Street House
4 Queen Street
Bath BA1 1HE

Produced by Magpie Books, an imprint of
Robinson Publishing Ltd, London

ISBN 1 90287 907 4

A copy of the British Library Cataloguing-in-Publication Data is available
from the British Library

Printed in China

ACKNOWLEDGEMENTS

Pictures on pp 3, 8, 13, 18, 20, 22, 49, 51, 52, 57, 60, 78, 80, 81, 82,
84, 86 and 87 are by courtesy of the National Museum of Ireland; that on
p 29 has been very kindly supplied by Mr Paul O'Hanlon. The picture on
p 65 from the *Book of Durrow* (Ms 57 folio 3v Carpet page with trumpet and
spiral decoration and six-ribbon interlacing) is by permission of Trinity
College Dublin/Bridgeman Art Library, London/New York

CONTENTS

introduction

N O ONE is sure when the first Celts arrived on the shores of Ireland. But everyone agrees that their exceptional skill and craftsmanship were somehow nurtured there. Soon they were to bring Ireland to the forefront of European art.

Two thousand years ago, Ireland was a place on the edge of the world. For centuries its isolation helped preserve the Celtic ways. Across the Irish Sea, British art was changing under the sway of the Romans. British craftsmen abandoned their supposedly barbaric tastes for "civilized" notions of beauty. Ireland, however, in Roman eyes, was too remote and savage a country to risk invading. The freedom from Roman influence allowed the Celts

to develop their unique and magical styles, their passion for the beauty of abstract shapes and symbols, and their delight in the minute intricacy of interweaving designs.

When the Roman Empire slowly began to collapse around the fifth century AD and Germanic hordes swept across Europe, the continent was shrouded in chaos, darkness and barbarism. But once again, Ireland was spared. It was not the Saxons, but Christianity that successfully breached the island. And through Christianity, the brilliance of a new creativity shone light into the soul of Irish art, expressed in masterpieces of metalwork and dazzling illuminated manuscripts.

Although untouched by the upheavals of Europe, that is not to say Celtic art existed in a vacuum. It survived invasions, migrations and conversion to a new religion. Indeed, their art would never have been what it was but for the many outside influences. The Irish Celts had a talent for picking out and manipulating the best of continental art while keeping the distinctiveness of their own art. They always managed to

Treasures of the Derrynaflan Hoard in the National Museum of Ireland

master new ideas without being mastered by them.

Even after the catastrophe of the Viking occupation from the ninth century onwards, the Celts recovered and achieved a second golden age. Monasteries were rebuilt, shrines remodelled. They appropriated Norse techniques and applied them to a range of glorious religious objects.

So we can trace the passage of their art, from the first rough stone sculptures of pagan deities, to the painstaking detail of the *Book of Kells*, to the lustrous austerity of the Cross of Cong. Individuality and originality were the hallmarks of the Celts. It was not until the Norman invasion of 1170 that their unique vision began to be destroyed. But in the centuries since, their art has remained celebrated throughout the world.

prehistory

HE earliest signs of human habitation in Ireland date back to about 7000 BC. Life then was a battle for survival, an unending search for food and shelter, a restless wandering over bogs and moors for plentiful hunting stocks. In fact, life was so difficult that it seems there was no time or thought for art. There is no trace, for example, of cave paintings such as those that had been drawn in France and Spain thousands of years before.

By the middle of the third millennium BC the nomadic way of life had largely ceded to small-scale settlements. Some included what have come to be known as "passage graves" or "passage tombs" – tomb chambers buried under

The entrance to Newgrange

a huge heap of stone and earth, only accessible by a slender passage from the edge of the mound. It is here that the first hints of a flourishing cultural life can be found.

Newgrange, on the river Boyne near Drogheda, is perhaps the most famous of the passage tombs, and is one of the most important prehistoric sites in the world. At the entrance to the passageway a great stone lies, decorated in two halves by whirling spirals, curls and arcs alongside boxes, diamonds, waves and zigzags. Beautiful as it may be, it is far more than just idle decoration. The single, neatly etched vertical line that separates each half marks the exact position of the winter solstice sunrise. Only then does the sunlight beam down the 20-metre passageway, flooding the tomb chamber within.

Academics believe that the ornamentation on the stones at the Newgrange site is art closely allied with an ancient astronomy in which solstices, seasons and phases of the moon were imbued with unearthly significance. The double-spirals in this carving are thought to mirror the movements of the sun's shadow wheeling one way in winter and the opposite in summer. Thus

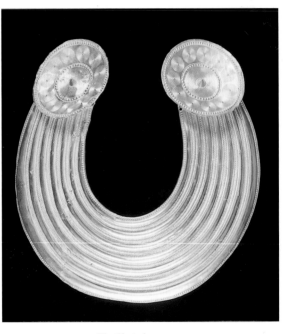

The Gleninsheen gorget

the artwork on the stone comes to depict the unfolding year.

Over the next 2000 years the art of carving on stones and boulders continued, particularly in the form of dots and concentric circles, much like the art found in Spain and Scotland, or spirals and waves, as in Brittany. These places would come to be centres of the Celtic world.

During this period, Ireland had also become something of a "land of gold", producing more gold jewellery than anywhere in prehistoric Europe. By about 800 BC there was a thriving industry in the south-west around the river Shannon, and goldsmiths employed a range of techniques to achieve the delicate effects manifested in pieces such as the Gleninsheen gorget, worn about the neck. The circular end-pieces, filled by many concentric circles, suggest contact with Northern Europe and the Iberian Peninsula, as do the stone etchings. Again, these are areas that the Celts had already penetrated.

The people responsible for this art were clearly very skilled and had travelled from areas in Europe often associated with the Celtic culture. However, although the recurring shapes and patterns in their artwork recall the Celtic styles of later centuries we cannot say with certainty that these were the first Celts in Ireland. What can be said is that when the people we know to be Celts stormed into Ireland at the start of the Iron Age they probably found that most of the inhabitants already spoke a language similar to their own Celtic tongue, the ancestor of Irish as it is spoken today.

the coming of the celts

AROUND 500 BC, the building of fortifications in Ireland is evidence of some sort of upheaval and unrest in the communities. Many think it was on account of the arrival of fierce hordes from the continent. It was these groups that effectively brought the Iron Age to Ireland, and their skill at working iron into swords and other armaments tipped the balance in their favour as they pushed across the island.

We cannot pinpoint exactly when these groups came, or indeed, whether they came at one time or in several waves, but we can say that they constituted the most significant influx of people known to be Celts to arrive in Ireland.

They travelled from central Europe through Gaul and Britain, perhaps squeezed from their homelands by the pressures of the expanding Roman civilization. These people were experts in metalwork and had developed a distinct style, named La Tène (meaning "the shallows") after a site revealed by the retreating waters of Lake Neuchâtel in Switzerland. La Tène art was characterized by swirling, sometimes floral lines and embellishments, perhaps ultimately derived from Ancient Greek motifs such as the honeysuckle. The La Tène style has become synonymous with early Celtic art.

The transformation to La Tène style was by no means a complete and instantaneous affair. For example, stone was still the favoured medium in many places, often sculpted into the images of Celtic deities rather than the decorative swirls of La Tène art. The stone double idol of Boa Island in County Fermanagh is one such object, featuring two figures carved back to back. Their hair fuses into a single criss-crossing whole and their short

(Opposite) The stone double idol of Boa Island

13

The Turoe stone

rigid arms protectively draw across their bodies while their wide eyes stare searchingly ahead. Idols such as this would have had strong symbolic and religious importance for the Celts; in many cases, the rock itself was thought to hold sacred powers before it had been sculpted.

But stone was soon being carved in an altogether different way. The Turoe stone, which stands in County Galway, is adorned with waxing and waning tendrils creeping over the granite, some blooming into little buds, others sprouting leaves or curling inwards. Here, too, can be seen one of the earliest appearances of the triskele, a three-legged shape within a circle, and trumpet-like forms, which come to occur with increasing frequency. The stone is, of course, not a represent-ation of a cult spirit as is the idol. Nevertheless, it was probably considered just as potent an object to the Celts who used it as part of their religion.

The abstract designs of the Turoe stone are emblematic of La Tène art. For many, the carving holds the properties of *repoussé* metalwork, beaten out from behind. This is no coincidence as the Celts were very accomplished smiths, taking delight in the balance and harmony of their work.

Iron provided new possibilities for weaponry and other equipment, and the Celts quickly took control of Ireland, aided by their superior arms. But the traditional metals, bronze and gold, were still very much the materials of preference for their artists. The Lisnacroghera scabbard, found with several other highly decorative scabbards in County Antrim, demonstrates the Celtic fervour for ornamentation on bronze. It dates from between the third and first centuries BC. Even with the confined space of the sword-sheath, the artist has created a pattern of wonderful control, engraving a hubbub of scrolls and trumpets against the peace of the untouched bronze. The result is careful poise between energy and tranquility, a perfect equilibrium.

At this time on the continent, Celtic art was faltering. The so-called "compass technique" had

been discarded there, whereas in Ireland it was in widespread use. The smiths that made the scabbards would have been experts in this technique, having practised over and over again on less valuable materials such as bone. Thousands of these "trial pieces" were recovered from a site in Lough Crew, County Meath, together with an iron object taken to be the arm of a compass. The compass would have been placed at different centres to draw regular curves of varying sizes. The resulting asymmetry creates a spontaneous, lively feel, while retaining a simple elegance and a subtle beauty.

A sumptuous hoard discovered in Broighter, County Derry, illustrates the Irish Celts' mastery of gold. Two very different treasures, dating from about the first century BC, show a

Engraved bone "trial piece" from Slieve-na Caillighe, County Meath

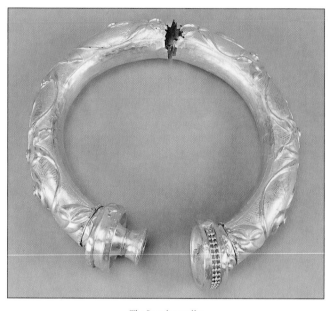

The Broighter collar

tremendous versatility of technique. The Broighter collar, a golden torc or neck ornament, resembles the carvings of the Turoe stone, but reaches a much higher level of craftsmanship. Swirling stems grow around the collar with buds of roses bursting into flower nearby. The gold-smith strove for a three-dimensional appearance to the design and enhanced the effect by roughening the background with a series of minute cross-hatchings. The sophisticated clasp mechanism to fasten the collar demonstrates how advanced Celtic metalwork had become.

The miniature gold boat, only 5cm high, was also found in the hoard. It would have been made as an offering to the gods of sea and water. The Celts believed that when they died the gods would carry them in a horse-drawn chariot to

Detail of the Broighter collar

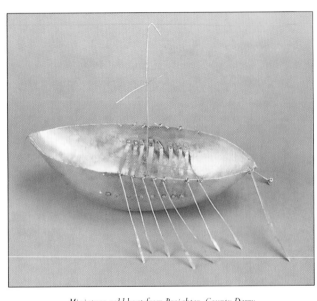

Miniature gold boat from Broighter, County Derry

the Otherworld far beneath the ocean. Perhaps this boat was an attempt to guarantee a king or nobleman's safe-passage in his journey there.

The Petrie Crown, named after its owner, George Petrie, a nineteenth-century archae-ologist, incorporates the elements associated with the "compass technique", although it was crafted using a different method. Made during the first two centuries AD, its delicate, curling trumpets mischievously mutate into bird and dragon heads, coloured bead-eyes burning red.

Animals, like the beasts of the Petrie Crown, recur throughout Irish Celtic art. Ownership of herd animals was an indication of wealth and status, so it stands to reason that the Celtic nobility would have wanted to see images of them in their art. Furthermore, the Irish Celts were keen horse-riders. About a quarter of all the surviving metalwork of the Iron Age on the island are horse-bits or horse-trappings. Many of these are also decorated with animal imagery.

By the time the Petrie Crown was made, much of Britain had already fallen to the Romans. To the Mediterranean invaders, the cold, wind-

The Petrie Crown

swept extremes of the island seemed like the edge of the Earth, the last outpost of where civilized life was possible. Little wonder that they were reluctant to venture still further from their homeland to Ireland, over a sea they thought as treacherous as any they had ever encountered. The Romans were never to set foot in Ireland. But their loss was most certainly Irish art's gain.

Ireland was probably the last Celtic stronghold to come into contact with the La Tène style. But it was also the place where it lived the longest. The Roman Empire was expanding over the continent, slowly suffocating the gentle charm of mainland Celtic art with naturalistic Classical ideas. But Irish art was left to breathe freely for centuries to come and its unique style flourished. So it was that Ireland alone would realize the ultimate possibilities of a culture dying elsewhere in Europe.

the christian awakening

ALTHOUGH the Celtic traditions in Ireland survived the rise and fall of the Roman Empire, very few artefacts of that time remain. It was not until Christianity touched Ireland in the fifth century that the Celtic artists were woken from their productive slumber. Curiously, the pieces from the beginning of the Christian era are so close in style to those of 400 years earlier that it was as if nothing had changed. The similarities have made it very difficult for experts to date some objects, and estimates of age often differ by centuries.

At least, on the surface it seemed that

nothing much had changed. But underneath, Christianity was transforming the way the Celts thought about their art. In place of a multitude of competing pagan spirits, the Celts were offered a unifying belief of a single God, a single focus towards which they could direct all their artistic energies. As the pagan world was being closed off, Christianity opened the door to a new universe of expression, of signs and symbols, of sacred objects, books and places of worship.

To understand fully the impact that Christianity had on Celtic art, we should spend a little time looking at how it took hold in Ireland and the way Celtic life was organized around it.

The conversion of the Celts to Christianity was a surprisingly peaceful affair. Rather than a violent overthrow of the old pagan order, the new religion was gently grafted on to everyday life. St Patrick was instrumental in spreading the faith, carefully sowing its seeds through the established ways, allowing it to grow without the sprinkling of a single martyr's blood.

St Patrick was born of a Romano-British

St Patrick's horn (based on a thirteenth-century manuscript)

family near Carlisle. In his youth he was captured by raiders from Ulster and forced into slavery, but he managed to escape to the continent. In 432 AD he returned, this time as a missionary driven by the ardour of his faith. Already familiar with the country, its language and its customs, he showed tolerance for the Celtic ways, adapting them where he could to arrive at a happy compromise between their old life and the new faith.

The druids gave way to him without much of a struggle, either abandoning or adapting their sacred sites according to Christian needs. Meanwhile St Patrick left behind him a series of bishoprics. This system had been devised in Roman society, where the city was the obvious focal point for religious organization. However, it was destined to fail as Ireland had a very different social structure, being without cities or even walled towns. Kings and chieftains ruled over their tribes in small territories. As an amalgamation of independent kingdoms, the Celtic tribal system had no centre, no great city and no large towns. There was no need for roads because there was nowhere to go.

Unsurprisingly, it was not long after St Patrick's death at the end of the fifth century that his network of town-based bishoprics collapsed. Instead, Christianity came to be practised in monasteries: a way far more appropriate to the isolated farms and villages of Celtic society, and far more beneficial to the development of Celtic art.

In the fifth century, the ascetic life of the monastery was becoming increasingly appealing throughout troubled Europe. As the power of Rome shrank and the belligerent Germanic tribes swept over the continent leaving chaos in their wake, the example set by St Anthony, who chose to follow an entirely spiritual life as a hermit in the scorching Egyptian desert, could not have been more attractive.

Ireland's remote and wind-battered coasts, too rocky to till and thoroughly comfortless, also held the unearthly qualities, the mystical beauty of St Anthony's desert. Monasticism was sure to thrive. Indeed, St Enda founded the first Irish monastery at Killeany on the Aran island of Inishmore, and by the end of the sixth century,

The ruins of the old monastery of Moville, said to have been founded by St Finnian

thanks to the zealousness of St Finnian of Clonnard, there were monasteries all over the country.

For Irish art the effect was profound. The monasteries became great centres of learning, the new cradles of art and literature. Providing peace and safety from the Anglo-Saxon invasion of England, they were a haven for many craftsmen fleeing the troubles. These metal-smiths and glassworkers introduced a variety of new skills to the Celts, such as the technique of millefiori glass (literally meaning "thousand flowers") whereby fused bundles of coloured glass rods of various sizes were cut into cross-sections. In metalwork, filigree began to appear, which involved the use of fine wire or grain to make intricate patterns on a metal surface. This can be seen on a tiny gold bird, no bigger than a thumb-nail, found in Garryduff in County Cork and dating from around the sixth century.

As the abbots of the monasteries superseded St Patrick's bishops in power and importance, the kings and chieftains (some of whom were wealthy enough to import olive oil and wine from the Mediterranean) were keen to associate with them. So the long-standing tradition of artistic patronage was preserved under the new religious order. Discoveries of artists" equipment, such as moulds and crucibles alongside sticks of millefiori glass inside the chieftains" fort-residences, or *raths*, shows the importance of these craftsmen in Celtic society.

(Opposite) folio 5r from the Book of Kells

31

The Irish monasteries also provided the basis for a widespread cultural exchange across Europe. The evangelical spirit drove Irish missionaries through the continent, until Ireland became famous for its artistic enlightenment and cultivation of learning. By the late eighth century, the Irish Celts were highly sought after as teachers, and King Charlemagne insisted on recruiting them. They set up monasteries across Europe, where Irish artists became familiar with a variety of new ideas and techniques. The missionaries christianized the Picts of Scotland and the Anglo-Saxons in northern England, setting up monasteries in Iona and Lindisfarne, where some of the greatest illuminated manuscripts were produced. In this way, Ireland was responsible for a kind of renaissance, taking a central role in the blossoming of a new artistic development in Europe.

In the next chapters we shall see how this injection of creativity brought about by Christianity affected art in Ireland.

CROSSES OF STONE

THE ascetics and hermits, who forswore all wealth and worldly power for the life of unswerving spiritual devotion, rarely even treated themselves to the luxury of a church. Instead they built crude stonework huts and oratories, as found at the rock of Skellig Michael near the Kerry coast. They were sparsely furnished with little more than a wooden altar pushed against a central slab that marked the grave of the founding saint.

These otherwise unremarkable slabs, however, were the origin of a long tradition of Celtic stone crosses. As we have seen, sacred stones like the Turoe stone had for centuries played a part in the pagan cults. St Patrick first marked

the changeover to Christianity on many of these stones by scratching crosses on them. This practice soon became widespread, but in its austere beginnings nothing more than a rough cross hewn into such a slab or pillar was deemed necessary to mark a holy place.

Towards the close of the seventh century, slabs and pillars, as if following a calling of their own, began to grow larger and were cut into more regular shapes.

The oratory at Gallurus

One of the earliest of these is the pillarstone at Kilnasaggart, County Armagh. Made just after 700 AD, the pillar reaches almost seven feet, with simple crosses carved into circles. Many of them feature Maltese-style crosses, such as the slabs of Inishkea, County Mayo, and Reask, County Kerry. Others bear the Chi-Rho monogram (the first two letters of Christ using the Greek alphabet) or representations of the Crucifixion itself as at Duvillaun, County Mayo.

Of about the same period, the Fahan Mura slab of Donegal stands nine feet high and is filled by a giant cross composed of elaborate knots and plaits. In the space around the cross's stem, two little figures shelter under the ribbons. On the other side two birds sit atop another cross and an inscription trumpets a Greek version of the *Gloria Patri*: "glory and honour to the Father and to the Son and to the Holy Ghost". Birds and figures are also prominent in carvings on slabs at Drumhallagh and Iniskeel also in Donegal.

In these examples the crosses are confined to the limits of the stone; although they develop in size and grandeur, as with the Fahan slab, they

Base of the cross at Tuam

have not yet broken free of this space. But before
long, the cross began to dominate the shape of the
actual monument. A defining moment is captured
in the Carndonagh cross, which stands a few
miles from the Fahan slab and is probably the
work of the same carvers. The ten-foot
monument marks the triumphant liberation of
the cross from the slab. Christ resplendent stands
in the centre, his head emphasized as if by a halo,
while around him seven figures worship. Above
there is a large cross of ribbons, while the reverse
side is wrapped in many interwoven bands.

Cross at Durrow

During the course of the eighth century the Irish stonecutters experimented with these various forms and began to move towards a standard type of decoration for the gardens and greens of monastery buildings. This was the high cross, now one of the most famous symbols of early Christian Ireland.

The high cross was not unique to Ireland. In fact they occurred in all parts of Britain, not to mention in the Armenian and Coptic civilizations of the Christian Near East. But the high crosses of Ireland have best survived the passage of time and are among the most beautifully carved.

A cross in a circle is a persistent motif of the Irish high crosses. The form was already in common use for processions and for altars, but made of metallic sheets beaten into interlaced ribbons and spirals, and hammered on to a wooden base. Unfortunately, no examples of these processional crosses remain.

The North cross at Ahenny, however, is a twelve-foot representation in stone of the missing wood and metal forms. The entire cross is loaded with ornamentation, as was normal for most

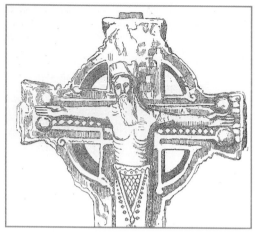

Head of the Tuam cross

metal versions. Other features reveal this cross's debt to contemporary metalwork. The rope mouldings at the edges of the monument copy an identical device employed to disguise the joints of separate bronze sheets. And its five lumpy bosses mimic the enamel or glass studs regularly used by metalsmiths to hide rivets.

A stylistic anomaly appears on the base of the cross – a depiction of a man under a palm tree, perhaps hunting or chasing a group of curious-looking animals. Similar tableaux appear on several Irish high crosses (for example, the Banagher pillar of County Offaly), yet they hold no place in the vocabulary of Celtic metalwork. They are probably derived from Late Roman artefacts, such as the Franks Casket, a Northumbrian ivory box, dating from the early eighth century, which is carved with hunting scenes, blending pagan and Christian signs. It seems reasonable to suggest that such carvings on Irish crosses may not carry a religious significance but are more a gesture to the artistic fashions of the time.

The Moone cross, County Kildare, is one of the strangest of the Irish high crosses. Stretching upwards from a thin, tapering base, it almost reaches 18 feet in length. Again, animals appear on the cross, but this time they are explicitly Christian, illustrating biblical events. Each side of the base tells a different story: on one we have

(Opposite) folio 7v from the Book of Kells

Adam and Eve, Abraham's attempted sacrifice of Isaac, and Daniel in the Lion's Den. Another side shows the miracle of the loaves and fishes, and the flight to Egypt. The biblical stories referred to here were very popular by the close of the eighth century, having come into circulation through the Irish religious literature of the Culdee reformist movement.

The cross also bears St Paul and St Anthony meeting in the desert, not a biblical scene as such, but being the patron saints of monastic life their inclusion is not surprising. One whole side of the pediment is taken up with the twelve apostles who stare at us cheerily, carved plainly with block bodies and pear-shaped heads. The shaft is decorated with creatures all the way to the cross itself, and at the top six giddy spirals spit out fearsome-looking beasts.

The Moone cross is particularly endearing for its charming simplicity. There is no fuss or clutter, but each figure, despite its naiveté, is powerfully alluring. To some the figures have the expressive quality of a child's picture-book. Indeed, crosses such as this may well have had a similar purpose, being used to portray Bible stories for those who could not read the Latin scriptures themselves.

The finest of all the Irish high crosses is found at Monasterboice in Louth. This was a centre for one of the most gifted schools of Celtic sculptors, who created the colossal cross of Muiredach. The precision of its carving has endured remarkably over a thousand years of wind and rain. Much of its crispness has been saved, even though it is made of sandstone. Some say that the shingle roof at the top of the cross, like those of contemporary Irish churches, helped to protect it.

Unlike the narrow cross of Moone, its wide shaft gives it an almost squat appearance in photographs and drawings. Nonetheless it is a few inches taller than Moone, and its breadth allows for scenes more expansive and detailed than any other cross. The lowest panel on the eastern face shows Eve tempting Adam with the forbidden fruit beneath the heavy boughs of the apple tree, and to their right, mankind's second sin: Cain's murder of Abel. Moving up, David stands victorious over a suppliant Goliath, and above them Moses smites the rock.

The main part of the cross displays Christ in Judgment, perhaps as vivid a scene as any on the high crosses. To His right, the saved approach Him, led by David and a little bird perched upon his harp. To His left, a man playing the panpipes coaxes the damned towards the devil, who rounds them up with his trident. At Christ's feet, the Archangel Michael is busy weighing souls. The devil has secreted himself below and with a long rod tries to tip the scales in his favour. All is not lost as St Michael battles for justice by shoving his staff deep down Satan's gullet.

Everything about the cross releases a rich flavour of the life in the Monasterboice community. The holy men bear Celtic croziers, while on the west face, the Arrest of Christ depicts not Roman soldiers but what appear to be moustachioed Viking warriors brandishing swords at His chest. The Viking invasions of the ninth century sent shock waves through Celtic society, so the sculptors are easily forgiven for replacing the Romans with another Godless

The high cross of Muiredach, Monasterboice

Detail of the Chi-Rho page of the Book of Kells *(folio 34r)*

civilization, however historically inaccurate. In this carving, Christ sports a brooch, an accessory that denoted status amongst the Celts. At His feet, two cats recall those on the famous Chi-Rho page of the *Book of Kells*.

References such as these fix the Irish high crosses in a fertile cultural world, a world full of vitality where stonemasons, metalsmiths, artists and scribes exchanged ideas, generating new styles that could be expressed in any medium. Perhaps the most influential craftsmen of all were the smiths, whose luxuriant work inspired everyone around them.

the golden age of celtic metalwork

BETWEEN the seventh and ninth centuries, Celtic art in Ireland reached its pinnacle. In this period, the Celts had developed the La Tène style to a new level. At the same time, an influx of foreign craftsmen introduced new techniques and themes, creating a fertile and potent mix of ideas. Out of this melting-pot were forged some of the finest ever examples of European Celtic metalwork, outstanding pieces of breathtaking technical expertise. This was the golden age of Celtic art.

Despite outside influence they still bear the mark of the Irish traditions. These are not

pastiches of the exotic or crude copies as some of the continental Celtic art had been in the Roman era. On the contrary, the Irish Celts selected and moulded imported ideas to suit their own passions, so producing unique and distinctly Celtic hybrid forms.

The Celtic gift for absorbing outside elements and slotting them into the old traditions is well demonstrated with the brooches. Penannular (literally meaning "almost a ring"), brooches had been used as cloak-fasteners in Ireland as early as the fifth century. They were simple objects, perhaps livened up with engravings at the ring-ends or terminals.

During the sixth and seventh centuries, the brooches grew more ostentatious: the fastening-pin doubled in length, the ring-ends joined to form an unbroken circle, while the terminals grew into triangular attachments large enough to accommodate thick decoration. Such showy objects must have been a badge of rank, a loud declaration of high social standing.

The silver brooch from Roscrea, County Tipperary, is an example of how expertly the

The silver brooch from Roscrea,
County Tipperary

Celtic jewellers adapted foreign techniques to their work. Saxon jewellery, which had been imported to Ireland throughout the seventh century, was admired for its glittering brilliance, its use of sparkling stones and light-reflecting filigree and engraving. The Irish metalsmiths were too discriminating merely to ape Saxon style, but picked only its best features and improved on them. Where the Saxons would have used garnets and big stones to draw the eye, the Celts found that simple contrast between minute decoration and unfilled space was more effective and less gaudy. The Roscrea Brooch is rich with detail, but offset by a clean, unadorned silver ring. The edges of the terminals appear plain too, but under close scrutiny rows of minute spirals flash into view.

The contrast and balance between the decorated and the plain, between light and dark, can also be seen in the bronze belt buckle of Lagore, County Meath. The ornamentation of the three-legged triskeles is set off by the shining metal on a black background. Such an effect was achieved by the chip-carving technique derived from woodworking. The metalsmith would have

cut a V-shaped groove into a casting mould, or etched directly into the metal to produce the arresting contrast. Here, enduring Celtic designs are represented by the swirling triskeles and roundel, while the only Saxon influence comes in the form of a tiny dog's head at the tapering end of the buckle.

The item comes from the royal crannog, an artificial fort-island built only a few miles from Tara, the legendary seat of the High Kings of Ireland. After Tara was destroyed, Lagore seems to have been the next royal home.

Heralded as the finest piece of all Celtic jewellery, the Tara Brooch was surely worthy of royalty. In truth, the brooch was not found at Tara, but named

The bronze belt buckle of Lagore

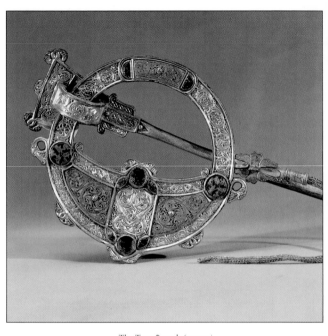

The Tara Brooch (reverse)

The Tara Brooch (front)

after the place because of its regal splendour. It was discovered in a wooden box on the beach at the mouth of the Boyne, near Bettystown, County Meath.

Every known technique of the time was used in its creation, such as engraving, filigree, casting and *intaglio*, the process of cutting an image in reverse relief below the surface of the metal. Enamel, moulded glass and amber were embedded in the gold against a silver-gilt backdrop of coiling beasts and birds, again inspired by Saxon art. Only in enlarged pictures is it possible to see the level of skill involved; for example, the filigree animals and interlacings are made up of the tiniest grains of metal.

Whoever wore it certainly would have treasured its exceptional decoration, not least the spectacular reverse side that only they could have seen as they took it on and off. We can only guess at the effect the brooch had on those who saw it, especially considering the presence of its silver chain, suggesting that it was one of a pair. Unfortunately, the chain has been severed, and the brooch's twin has never come to light.

Even the chain attachment is a small wonder. It is joined to the body of the brooch at each side by the clenched jaws of two dragons, recalling the grand door-knocker of Donore, County

Meath. Between the dragons lie two diminutive glass beads, moulded into human faces. These individual details standing alone show the jeweller's virtuosity. Extraordinarily, they also work as parts of a whole, combining as one to form the head of a snake, with the glass beads as its eyes and the meandering chain its tail.

The front and back of the brooch conjure quite different moods. The front is refined and sophisticated. The filigree patterns inlaid with coloured glass and amber seem to confirm the wearer's stateliness. Whereas the back teems with life, a menagerie of contorting animals that wrestle and writhe, battling for a way out of the panels that confine them.

The Tara Brooch embodies the perfect selection and combination of foreign designs and techniques. Dating from the early eighth century it marks the peak of Irish metalwork. Ornamental brooches continued to be produced well into the ninth century. Some repeated aspects of the Tara Brooch's animal imagery, others incorporated floral themes, such as the thistle, which was a popular Viking motif. But none surpassed the artistry and magnificence of the Tara Brooch.

One object survives that does capture the finesse of the Tara Brooch. The Ardagh Chalice belongs to roughly the same period, the early eighth century, and some claim it could have come from the same workshop, even perhaps by the same hand. The outstanding quality of the two pieces places them some distance above the rest, rousing suspicion that they are connected.

The chalice was unearthed from a field in 1868 by a young boy digging up potatoes at Ardagh, County Limerick. It shows more restraint than the Tara Brooch, with explosions of gold tempered by stretches of plain silver. Below an undecorated rim runs a band of fine gold filigree punctuated by ten red and blue glass studs, each one incorporating an inlaid cross. Beneath this, the names of the Apostles are delicately etched into the silver. Despite these religious connotations, the chalice is not thought to have been used in church. Rather, these features are a gesture towards Christianity, and the object was pure decoration, for the pleasure of some king to show off and enjoy.

The Ardagh Chalice

Each face of the chalice is marked by a golden circle dotted with glass studs and gentle filigree spirals. Under the broad handles, which are fashioned in red, blue and green, the large enamel studs are so greatly embossed that they stand out over half an inch from the bowl. The effect of enamel with inlaid metal was achieved by placing the desired pattern, usually made of bronze, upside down in a mould. The appropriate colour of enamel would then be poured into the separate compartments. This technique was borrowed from the Saxons but is very seldom seen in Irish work.

An oddity of the piece is on the underside of the base, only visible by raising the chalice above one's head. Spirals, triskeles and squirming animals rotate around a central rock crystal. The use of such ornamental stone was again very rare in Ireland.

The stem of the chalice is bronze with heavy gilding, decorated with the most accomplished and intricate filigree patterns. The technical skill needed to make this section far transcends anything known from Saxon metalwork. Some go further, proclaiming it as the finest example of filigree work of any age.

The quality of the Ardagh Chalice is so high, with its careful balance between youthful exuberance and understated grandeur, that it has earned a place among the greatest of all Early Christian metalwork.

So far we have looked at secular pieces, but monasteries also required metalwork for shrines and book covers. The bronze Rinnagan Crucifixion Plaque, County Roscommon was one such book cover. It is likely to be a little older than the Ardagh Chalice, and much of its design is firmly rooted in the Celtic art of pagan times. It is also one of the first representations of the Crucifixion in Irish Art.

In this piece, no respect is paid to proportion. The plaque's emphasis is on drawing attention to the Glory of Christ. It is His face that dominates the cover. The bulging oval eyes, the slit-mouth and the stylized hair of all the figures strongly recall the sacred stone idols of many centuries earlier. The hems of Christ's clothing are adorned with linked spirals, while His body is resplendent

The bronze Rinnagan Crucifixion Plaque, County Roscommon

with whorls and curved and angular interlacing. In every respect, Christ appears as a Celt.

Above Him winged angels hover, their undersized legs dangle in the air giving the impression of flight. Below His arms, Stephaton and Longinus, the characters who offered Christ a sponge of vinegar and pierced him with a lance, crane their heads mournfully backwards.

The figures and decoration are very like those of the contemporary illuminated manuscripts. It is probable that the artist was familiar with such scenes and moved enough by them to offer similar versions in metal. The influence of the manuscripts did not stop with local artists. In truth, these written works were so exquisite that they inspired artists throughout Europe.

the word of god

WITH no type of art did the new-found Church have greater influence than the illuminated manuscripts. The inspiration to decorate manuscripts came from faraway places through a network of monasteries that Irish monks had founded on the continent.

The first missionaries left Ireland to spread the new faith around the middle of the fifth century. They built monasteries in the British Isles and on the continent, founding great centres of learning and artistry. In 613, St Gall set up one of the most influential monasteries, at Bobbio in Northern Italy. It was here that the Irish monks first saw the beautiful illuminated

manuscripts from the east, particularly Coptic scripts. The Copts were Christians of Egypt, who decorated their texts with dots and interlacing designs, features which later appeared in Irish works.

The travelling monks and missionaries kept in close contact with their homeland, ferrying interesting and inspirational texts to Ireland. Before long the Coptic designs were adapted by the Celtic monks to decorate their own manuscripts.

The *Book of Durrow* is one of the earliest and finest of the surviving Irish manuscripts, written in the late seventh century. It is a copy of the Gospels and for centuries belonged to the monastery founded by St Columba at Durrow, County Offaly. When the monastery was dissolved in the seventeenth century, it found its way into the hands of a local farmer, who used it to cure his sick cattle by dipping it into their drinking water. Fortunately it was rescued and given to Trinity College, Dublin.

Inside we see the influence of the Coptic texts, namely the devotion on an entire page to decoration, termed a "carpet page". The manuscript opens with a page bearing a double cross, followed by one with the symbols of the four Evangelists. Before each Gospel is a symbol of the Evangelist and a beautifully painted carpet page. The text of each Gospel begins with an embellished initial letter, sometimes sprouting rapacious-looking beasts.

It is probably the first Irish manuscript to use several colours. Four colours are used – dark green, brilliant yellow, deep red and pale brown – and they contrast wonderfully against the rich black-brown shade of the vellum pages. Bearing in mind the size of the book at only $9\frac{1}{2}$ x $6\frac{1}{2}$ inches, not much larger than a standard paperback, the precise ultra-fine lines and the accuracy of decoration are stunning.

On one carpet page (folio 3v), the rhythm and arrangement of the colours on a black background produces a very full and vibrant effect – a great feat, considering the limited palette available. The space around the designs

(Opposite) Carpet page (folio 3v) from the Book of Durrow

has been darkened and is left uncluttered, adding to the overall sense of balance and restraint. Here, too, the familiar Celtic spirals and whirls (very like those of the Turoe stone) crop up alongside a feature imported from the east: interlaced bands. This element, of Coptic origin, was one of the most important acquisitions of the Celtic artists. As we have seen, these patterns, originally from the manuscripts, were picked up by the masons and metalsmiths, and developed through Celtic traditions into increasingly complicated patterns.

Another extraordinary carpet page, (folio 192v), features interlaced bands of animals. In a teeming mass of life, their long jaws clamp about their neighbours" bodies, or where that is not possible, bite on their own legs and tails. Many animal ornaments came from Saxon and Nordic origins, but none of these ancestral works came anywhere near the ingeniousness of their Celtic offspring. The rhythm and compositional clarity of this page is of an entirely Celtic pedigree.

In the middle design a Maltese cross marks

the centre of a triangle made up of three circles with stepped crosses inside, which may represent the Holy Trinity. The designs of these circles closely resemble the grilled enamel studs of the Ardagh Chalice fifty years later. But we should remember that the first Celts that came to Ireland were fine metalsmiths and the cross-fertilization of ideas went both ways. The symbol of St Matthew (folio 21v) confirms this. His cloak contains hundreds of contrasting squares, exactly like the millefiori patterns found on escutcheons dated from centuries earlier.

In the hundred years following the completion of the *Book of Durrow*, the decorations on the Irish manuscripts were becoming ever more elaborate, involving intricate ornaments and complex animal motifs all rendered in a number of colours. Several books of this period have survived, but it has proved difficult to trace their

origins. Books were easily moved, and colophons (inscriptions placed at the end with the production details) often altered or erased. It does appear that some, such as the *Book of Lindisfarne*, the *Book of Lichfield* and the *St Gall Gospels* were written outside Ireland, doubtless by Celtic scribes and illuminators at Irish monasteries. The skill and artistry of these volumes was perfected in the *Book of Kells*, the supreme accomplishment of Irish Celtic art, and perhaps the world's greatest illuminated manuscript.

The *Book of Kells* has a chequered past. The manuscript was started in the monastery founded by St Columba on the Scottish island of Iona. When the Vikings invaded the island around 800, the monks quickly spirited it away to the relative safety of Ireland. Here its 370 folios (740 pages) were completed at another Columban monastery in Kells, County Meath. The Annals of Ulster tell how in 1007, the book, the "chief relic of the western world" was "wickedly stolen in the night", only to be recovered a few months

(Opposite) folio 33r from the Book of Kells

69

ҺGENERATIO

later from under a sod of earth. Its gold ornamentation had been stripped.

In the 339 folios that have survived, we see not only the seamless fusion of the many elements that then comprised Celtic art, but also their sublime perfection. Forty full-page illustrations, painted in an array of colours, demonstrate the mastery of several artists, one of whom has been called "the Goldsmith", the painter of two of the most breathtaking pages. The Eight-Circled Cross (folio 33r) is a miracle of design and intricate ornamentation. The book was a luxury to be placed open on the altar and pages such as this must have left churchgoers reeling from wonder and delight.

The other of the Goldsmith's creations stands out above all the other pages. Known as the Monogram page, or Chi-Rho page (folio 34r), because it consists of the first two Greek letters of "Christ", it has been called "the most elaborate page of calligraphy ever executed". The page demonstrates all the motifs present in Celtic art of

(Opposite) folio 34r from the Book of Kells

that time: firstly the abstract, such as the knots, interlaced bands, triskeles and spirals; secondly the figures from nature – birds, fish, foliage and the fantastic beasts. To these it adds human forms, a recognition of Christ's centrality to Celtic beliefs. In fact, unlike the *Book of Durrow*, portrait pages occur throughout the manuscript, with represent-ations of Christ, his Apostles, the Evangelists, angels and even the devil.

The decoration of the Chi-Rho page is so dense that at first it is almost baffling. On some portions the ornamentation is practically in-visible without a magnifying glass. But the minute detail is so expertly blended into the graceful sweep of the "chi" letter and the overall concept of the page that its magnificence is never diminished. The playful animal scenes at the bottom of the page – cats and mice, and an otter chomping on a fish – add a touch of humour and ground the other-worldly artistry in everyday life.

Wit and imagination abound in the *Book of*

Initial letters from the Book of Kells

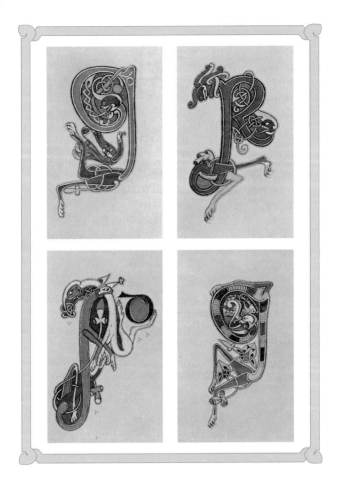

Kells. Initial letters throughout the manuscript employ zoomorphic (animal-like) forms. Often a ravenous mouth opens to spew forth a sinuous tongue, which entwines around the animal's body. Sometimes they bite the neck of another monstrous beast and their linked bodies make up the initial. The Genealogy of Christ page (folio 200r) shows a succession of initial "q"s, each joined to the next by a dog holding a bird's throat in its teeth.

The *Book of Kells* represents Irish Celtic art at its best. The numerous artistic influences, from Scandinavia to Egypt, are happily married on the pages of the manuscript. Previously exotic forms had become so familiar to the Irish scribes that they no longer appeared as borrowings, but were fully subsumed into the Celtic tradition. These illuminators painted with such skill and confidence that the Irish Celtic style travelled back to the continent, itself influencing European book illumination for centuries to come.

the twilight of celtic art

THE Vikings first made raids on Ireland at the end of the eighth century. They came in waves, working their way around the coasts in their longboats, sacking and plundering the monasteries, melting down the silver and gold ornaments into coins. Manuscripts were destroyed without a thought and the great illuminators and metalsmiths took flight to the continent. The marauding pagans shocked Christian Ireland to its core.

Celtic art was obviously popular among the invaders as much of what survives today was recovered from excavated Scandinavian graves.

But the upheaval caused by the invasions seems to have taken its toll on the quality of metalwork from the ninth and tenth centuries. For example, the brooches, which were still fashionable at this time, were mostly poor imitations of previous work. Filigree decoration became cruder, while interlacing lacked its earlier brilliance. Of course, we should remember that many of the era's best pieces could have been destroyed.

It was not until the turmoil of the period had subsided, marked in part by Brian Boru's defeat of the Vikings at the Battle of Clontarf in 1014, that the old glory of Celtic metalwork was re-kindled. Only then did the Viking city of Dublin come into harmony with Irish ways, after its conversion to Christianity. Scandinavian and Celtic craftsmen began working side by side for a common religious purpose. As the Viking danger

ended, their art-forms became increasingly fashionable to the Celts. And with many new converts, the monasteries began to rebuild their wealth and could afford to open workshops devoted to the production of religious objects.

The Irish and Scandinavian styles had much in common and were mutually appealing. Soon both groups of craftsmen were sharing their knowledge and pooling their skills to make shrines and other ecclesiastical pieces. So Irish art enjoyed a resurgence, and many splendid pieces were produced.

Long before this time the notion of venerating relics had been well established in Ireland. Bones and personal objects of the saints were thought to hold the power to bless the living, or even the dead buried near a reliquary. The relics were important parts of Irish life, being paraded in processions, conferring gravity on special occasions, used for swearing oaths; they were even taken into battle as a kind of military ensign. Books were also venerated. Special holy objects such as these were often kept in ornate shrines, which could only contribute further to an object's solemnity.

With the artistic collaboration between the Celts and the Norse settlers, many old shrines were remodelled with a new look, a more Viking look. The book-shrine of the Gospel of St Molaise, known as the Soiscél Molaise, is a good example of this, produced at the beginning of the eleventh century. It depicts the symbols of the four Evangelists with their names etched into the compartments framing them. The filigree knotwork is still below the standard of the Tara Brooch, but the four figures have a fresh, vibrant, lively feel about them.

The book-shrine of St Maelruain's Gospel, otherwise known as "the shrine of the Stowe Missal" was made a generation later. The decoration on the top, including the great gems and rock-crystals, are medieval, but the rest is eleventh century. The figures on the side panels are similar in character to those of the Soiscél Molaise and resemble tenth century sculptures. One panel shows a harpist and an angel next to two clerics with a crozier and a bell. Some are

(Opposite) The Soiscél Molaise

The shrine of the Stowe Missal

The Breac Maodhóg

embellished with small studs of blue glass.

The castings of saints in bronze from a shrine known as the Breac Maodhóg are truly unique. The patterns around the borders are not of the

82

Celtic tradition. However, the folds of the figures" garments and the luxuriance of their hair recall the earlier Irish manuscripts. It remains a mystery exactly who the figures represent or even how the panels were displayed on the shrine.

The Scandinavian styles really come to the fore in Irish art between about 1090 and 1140. Made at the beginning of this period, the wonderfully ornate Shrine of St Patrick's Bell has a network of zoomorphic interlacings, a typical motif of the Norse styles. This time the creatures are no more than threads, occasionally offering an unblinking, bulbous eye of glass and long, distended jaws. The threads curl and coil in diagonals with pleasing rhythm. Some lost panels of gold filigree have been replaced by large quartz crystals, which detract a little from the effect of such fine metalwork. The shrine still contains "the sweet-sounding bell of St Patrick", for centuries the object of great veneration in the monastery of Armagh.

Fortunately, several croziers from around this

(Opposite) The Shrine of St Patrick's Bell

period have survived. Some only come to us in fragments, others in their entirety. The Clonmacnoise Crozier of the early twelfth century is one of the more intact. Scandinavian influence can be seen in many places, not least the animal head on the nub of the crook. The most striking feature is the winding silver snakes edged with black niello (a dark paste used as a metal inlay) slithering all over the crook, intertwined with a criss-cross of thin, budding tendrils. The technique needed to achieve this was also borrowed from the Norse settlers, and allowed a creative freedom till then unknown by Celtic metalworkers. The Celts applied it to these fantastic interlacings, providing a seemingly endless mass of knots and lines. As always with Celtic art, there is a strict logic to the apparent disorder.

One of the best-preserved sacred objects of this time is the Shrine of St Lachtin's arm. Very similar to the Clonmacnoise Crozier in style, this shrine again uses silver bands set into bronze, emphasized with black strips of niello.

(Opposite) The Clonmacnoise Crozier.

The knotwork is even tighter and more fanciful than the crozier, and once more, slender creatures creep and crawl between each other, sometimes raising a bellicose head to bark or bite. Wind-ruffled leaves and branches curl around the palm, and above them only the silver nails are kept free from decoration. The shrine has often been praised for the austere unity of its ornamentation, probably because of the small number of techniques used in its construction.

The masterpiece of twelfth century Irish metalwork, however, is the glorious Cross of Cong. It was made in 1123 under the orders of the High

(Opposite page) The Cross of Cong
(Left) The Shrine of St Lachtin's arm

87

King, Turlough O'Connor, to house a fragment of the True Cross. The relic was probably encased behind the crystal at the centre of the cross. The faces of the cross are divided into panels which bear peculiar long-legged beasts with minuscule heads entangled with combative, writhing snakes. These features are again of Scandinavian descent, but there is much about the cross that recalls the great Celtic pieces of the eighth century. For example, panels of fine filigree spirals revolve around the central crystal, while on the back, enamel studs are reminiscent of the Ardagh Chalice.

Most peculiar of all is the dragon that grips the base of the cross in its jaws. The two-sided monster bristles with scales, keeping ever-alert with large, open ears and watchful, blue glass eyes. Slightly pagan in feel it may be, but here its task is a holy one: to carry the cross at all times, to prevent its desecration by human touch.

In the Cross of Cong the rich ornamentation so characteristic of the Celts is laid out with uncharacteristic constancy. The riotous exuberance of earlier work has been controlled, yielding to a more disciplined expression of reverence. A wind of change was blowing through the Irish Church at that time, and with reform came a more solemn art. Although testaments to the enduring distinctiveness of Irish Celtic art, the shrines, crosses and croziers of this final period reflect a new sobriety. This was perhaps the last transformation of Celtic art.

For, in 1170, the Anglo-Norman invasion swept traditional Celtic art away. It was not a question of the Celts being wiped out or their art being suppressed by tyrannical conquerors. The Normans were absorbed into Ireland and Irish ways like the Vikings before them. But the new invaders opened the gates wider than ever before to a flood of continental culture that first eroded and then engulfed the native Irish styles. Bit by bit the art changed, until it was no longer possible to make out the features or feel of the great old Celtic artefacts.

For so long Ireland had been the last stronghold of Celtic art, and finally the stronghold had fallen.

Over 800 years later the achievements of

Celtic art are still potent symbols of Irish nationhood. And its spirit still endures, long outliving the culture that produced it. For today, in our streets, shops, pubs and books, on our clothes, coins, jewellery, cards, even tattoos, an art exists that is instantly recognizable as the legacy of the Irish Celts.